Towhead and the Little Yellow Kitten

Helen L. Merrell & Rita K. Fisher

To order additional copies of this book, contact:
Xlibris
1-888-795-4274
www.Xlibris.com
Orders@Xlibris.com

ISBN: Softcover   978-1-7960-7172-6
        EBook   978-1-7960-7173-3

Print information available on the last page

Rev. date: 11/15/2019

This story is dedicated to my daughter, Rita K. Fisher, for her love and devotion to me. It has carried me through many a trying time.

Acknowledgment

I want to thank two of my very dear friends, Lynn Flint and Helen Klippel. They very willingly gave their time and talent to make sure my dream for this book would come true.

Mother was in the kitchen drinking her second cup of coffee. Dad was in the barn doing his morning milking. Dad was a dairy farmer, and he had a large herd of Holstein milk cows. They were milked twice a day. The family's income came weekly from the creamery that purchased the milk. A truck picked up the milk daily and took it to the creamery, where it was made into cottage cheese, ice cream, and other milk products. A check would come weekly to pay the family's household expenses.

Mother also had an egg business of her own. She sold a crate of eggs to a local restaurant every week. This gave her grocery money and money to help with other expenses.

* * *

It was a beautiful morning. School was out for the summer vacation. Summer had finally arrived, and it was bringing warm, sunny days again. Towhead and Sammy were out playing basketball in the yard. Dad had made a basketball court for him to play in, and he practiced every day. He averaged six out of ten baskets. Towhead had a secret dream—that he would be able to play on his school's basketball team in a couple of years.

Suddenly, Towhead said, "Listen, Sammy, did you hear something?"

"Meow meow."

"There it was again, Sammy."

Sammy sniffed around, looking down at a patch of tall grass.

"Woof woof," Sammy barked.

"What is it? Get back and let me see what you've got. Why, it looks like a yellow piece of cotton." He bent down and picked it up and said, "Why, it is a little yellow kitten." He put it close to his face. "It is so soft. I wonder where it came from."

"Meow meow."

"Don't cry, little kitten. I'll take care of you. I wonder where your mama is. Maybe we can find her."

"Come on, Sammy, let's go show her to Mother. Maybe she'll let us keep her. She's so cute, and I've never had a kitten before." Towhead put the little yellow kitten in his pocket, and they hurried up to the house, just as fast as his little legs could carry them.

They found Mother sitting at the kitchen table; she was looking at a recipe book, wondering what to fix for supper.

"Hi, Mom, what are you doing today?"

"Well, hi, son. Today is my Red Hat meeting day, and I'm going to have a luncheon for them. Is it warm out?"

"Yes," said Towhead, "and I bet you cannot guess what I have in my pocket."

"Well, maybe it's a flower or a rock. I hope it's not a frog."

Towhead said, "It is not a frog."

Just then, the kitten started to cry *meow meow* as if to say "I want my mama. I am hungry. Meow meow."

Mother let out a loud cry, "What's that I hear? I hope it's not a cat! If it is, you get that out of here right now. I have enough to do without taking care of a cat boarder too!"

Towhead turned around crying and said, "Come on, Sammy. Let's get out of here." And they both ran out of the house as fast as their little legs could carry them, taking them into the barn lot and into the barn.

Towhead helped Sammy up into the haymow. Crying, Towhead said, "I've never heard my mother talk to me like that before. I can't believe it." He took the little yellow kitten out of his pocket, and he said, "Don't you worry. I'll take care of you. This old barn will make a nice home for you, and I'll bring you half my supper every night."

As they were exhausted, and with the kitten lying on Towhead's chest, the three of them fell asleep in the haymow.

When Dad came in from the barn, he found Mother crying. He put his arms around her and asked her, "What's the matter? Are you all right? Where is Towhead? Is he okay?"

"I'm such a bad mother. I just talked terribly to Towhead. I'm so ashamed. I must find him."

Mother told Dad how she was so nasty to Towhead and how loud she yelled at him for bringing home a little yellow kitten.

"I am so sorry. I must find him and tell him how sorry I am."

Dad said, "Now calm down. Things can't be that bad. Where is he now?"

Mother said, "I don't know. I haven't seen him since he ran out of the house upset with me."

"We'll go find him. He can't be so very far away on those little feet of his."

They looked and looked and called all close neighbors. It seemed like no one had seen him. Mother was so upset she began to cry again, thinking of the nasty way she had treated Towhead.

Mother and Dad had looked and called for over an hour. She wished she had been nicer to Towhead when he brought the kitten in.

Dad said, "I'll bet I know where he is." He was remembering that when he was a little boy, he always went to the haymow when he was upset and wanted to run away from home. "Let's look in the haymow. I bet you we will find him there."

Dad helped Mom up the ladder into the haymow. Sure enough, Dad was right. Towhead was holding the kitten in his lap, and he was fast asleep with Sammy and the little yellow kitten..

Mother could not control the happy tears as they ran down her cheeks. "I have never seen a more beautiful picture than the one I'm looking at right now," she said. "How could I ever think a kitten could be so much trouble to care for? Mothers are supposed to teach by actions. I'll never forgive myself."

When Mother reached out to Towhead, he opened his eyes with a look of fright. "Oh, please don't hurt my little yellow kitten."

"Oh, son, please forgive me," said Mother. "I could never hurt your kitten, son. Of course, I'll help take care of the little kitten."

Dad said, "A little yellow kitten can't be that much trouble to take care of. Why don't we make this a family project? I will make a little square box and fill it with sand and show you how to use it. It is called a litter box. Son, it'll be your job to take care of it. The only way the cat stays depends on how well you take care of it. Mother, your job is to see that the kitten has proper food and health care."

Mother said, "I don't think we should keep calling her little kitten. She needs to have a name."

"I think we should call her Sunshine," said Towhead. "She's yellow, and sunshine makes me happy."

"I'll go for that," Dad said.

So that's how Sunshine became a part of the family. Even Sammy seemed to like her. They all laughed every time Sunshine tried to bat Sammy's tail when she wiggled it.

As days turned into years, Sunshine became a beautiful, longhaired cat. And Mother found out that a cat in the house was more joy than care. Mother treated her like a baby, and she wondered how she ever could have thought a cat in the home could be so much trouble.

Sunshine loved to go to the barn during milking time. She would sit beside Dad, waiting for him to squirt some warm milk fresh from the cow into her open mouth when she was saying *meow meow* as if to say thank you. It was so funny to watch Sunshine sit beside Dad.

Towhead would still take Sammy and Sunshine to the haymow and take a nap. He said, "Sammy, I guess I'm the luckiest boy in the world to have you and Sunshine and a wonderful mother and dad. I thank God for being so good to me."

Printed in the United States
By Bookmasters